FACT or FICTION?

DO DRAGONS EXIST?

PETER FINN

Gareth Stevens Publishing

Please visit our website, www.garethstevens.com. For a free color catalog of all our high-quality books, call toll free 1-800-542-2595 or fax 1-877-542-2596.

Library of Congress Cataloging-in-Publication Data
Names: Finn, Peter, 1978- author.
Title: Do dragons exist? / Peter Finn.
Description: New York : Gareth Stevens Publishing, [2023] | Series: Fact or fiction? | Includes index.
Identifiers: LCCN 2021055111 (print) | LCCN 2021055112 (ebook) | ISBN 9781538280737 (Library Binding) | ISBN 9781538280713 (Paperback) | ISBN 9781538280720 (Set) | ISBN 9781538280744 (eBook)
Subjects: LCSH: Dragons–Juvenile literature. | Dragons–Folklore–Juvenile literature.
Classification: LCC GR830.D7 F58 2023 (print) | LCC GR830.D7 (ebook) | DDC 398.24/54–dc23/eng/20220105
LC record available at https://lccn.loc.gov/2021055111
LC ebook record available at https://lccn.loc.gov/2021055112

Published in 2023 by
Gareth Stevens Publishing
29 E. 21st Street
New York, NY 10010

Designer: Sheryl Kober
Editor: Therese Shea

Photo credits: Cover (top) and p. 1 Refluo/Shutterstock.com; cover and p. 1 (middle fire texture) Ron Dale/Shutterstock.com; cover and p. 1 (bottom image) T Studio/Shutterstock.com; pp. 1–32 (parchment background texture) Nella/Shutterstock.com; pp. 1–32 (sidebar background texture) Jojo Textures/Shutterstock.com; back cover and pp. 2–32 (It's A Fact background texture) Tawat Kambum/Shutterstock.com; p. 3 Susanitah/Shutterstock.com; p. 4 pavila /Shutterstock.com; p. 5 (top) crazy82/Shutterstock.com; p. 5 (bottom) Lakeview Images/Shutterstock.com; p. 6 Kuco/Shutterstock.com; p. 7 (top) Lefteris Papaulakis/Shutterstock.com; p. 7 (bottom) Alanstix64/Shutterstock.com; p. 8 (top) A.Sych/Shutterstock.com; p. 8 (bottom) dwi putra stock/Shutterstock.com; p. 9 Daniel Eskridge/Shutterstock.com; p. 10 Algol/Shutterstock.com; p. 11 carlos 401/Shutterstock.com; p. 12 ron and joe/Shutterstock.com; p. 13 delcarmat/Shutterstock.com; p. 14 (top) pavila/Shutterstock.com; p. 14 (bottom) https://en.wikipedia.org/wiki/Beowulf#/media/File:Beowulf_Cotton_MS_Vitellius_A_XV_f._132r.jpg; p. 15 Chonnanit/Shutterstock.com; p. 16 Vera She/Shutterstock.com; p. 17 (top) VladyslaV Travel photo/Shutterstock.com; p. 17 (bottom) Kuco/Shutterstock.com; p. 18 Ryujin https://en.wikipedia.org/wiki/Ry%C5%ABg%C5%AB-j%C5%8D#/media/File:Urashima_Taro_handscroll_from_Bodleian_Library_5.jpg; p. 19 (top) stockt0_0/Shutterstock.com; p. 19 (bottom) SYUNIMU/Shutterstock.com; p. 20 (top) Cube29/Shutterstock.com; p. 20 (bottom) Daniel Eskridge/Shutterstock.com; p. 21 (top) clicksdemexico/Shutterstock.com; p. 21 (bottom) Wangkun Jia/Shutterstock.com; p. 22 Kuko/Shutterstock.com; p. 23 (top) Warpaint/Shutterstock.com; p. 23 (middle) https://en.wikipedia.org/wiki/Zhenyuanlong#/media/File:Zhenyuanlong.jpg; p. 23 (bottom) Catmando/Shutterstock.com; p. 24 (top) BolshieBufera/Shutterstock.com; p. 24 (bottom) Jolygon/Shutterstock.com; p. 25 (top) Maynard Case/Shutterstock.com; p. 25 (middle) Kjersti Joergensen/Shutterstock.com; p. 25 (bottom) Kristian Bell/Shutterstock.com; p. 26 Kuko/Shutterstock.com; p. 27 Tithi Luadthong/Shutterstock.com; p. 28 ekatheartist/Shutterstock.com; p. 29 Melkor3D/Shutterstock.com; p. 29 nicku/Shutterstock.com.

Printed in the United States of America

CPSIA compliance information: Batch #CSGS23: For further information contact Gareth Stevens, New York, New York, at 1-800-542-2595.

CONTENTS

Words in the glossary appear in **bold** type the first time they are used in the text.

JUST MYTHS?

Tales about dragons are told all over the world. Some stories describe dragons as murderous and cruel. Others show them as protectors of humankind. Some dragons breathe fire. Others grant wishes and give gifts.

Cultures around the world include dragon myths and legends as part of their recorded history, bringing together fact and fiction. Some of the earliest stories about dragons came from Babylon and Egypt. Ancient Egyptians, for example, believed that the sun god Re defeated a dragon-like beast called Apopis each night.

This book will introduce you to more dragons of myth and **lore**. They range in size, ability, color, and **temperament**. So many stories from so many peoples exist that you have to wonder: Are dragons real?

DRAGONS OF BABYLON

In Babylonian stories, Tiamat was a dragon goddess of salt water. She gave birth to all the Babylonian gods. Another creature of Babylonian myth was mušḫuššu. It had a scaly dragon's body, the legs of a lion, a long neck and tail, and an eagle's **talons**. It was a symbol of the god Marduk and was featured on the Ishtar Gate, which was built during the time of King Nebuchadnezzar II, around 575 BCE.

The Ishtar Gate of ancient Babylon was decorated with images of dragons. This reconstruction is in Berlin, Germany. An illustration of the city and gate is below.

IT'S A FACT!

Babylon was a famous ancient city. It was the capital of southern Mesopotamia, an area of southwestern Asia between the Tigris and Euphrates Rivers.

DRAGONS IN EUROPE

The dragons of European legends were enormous animals with reptilian, or reptile-like, bodies. Some had two legs, and others had four. Some had wings, and some could breathe fire. They killed with their sharp talons and teeth. Most dragons had only one head, but the dragon Typhon had one hundred!

In Greek myths, Typhon was the youngest son of Gaea, the Earth goddess, and Tartarus, the god of the **underworld**. In some stories, Zeus, the ruler of the gods, threw Typhon into the underworld. In other tales, the many-headed dragon was imprisoned under Mount Etna on the island of Sicily. Mount Etna isn't a myth—it's an actual volcano. Ancient Greeks sometimes blamed Typhon for making it erupt! It was a way to explain a confusing natural event.

IT'S IN THE *ILIAD*

The *Iliad* is a famous Greek **epic**. According to tradition, the poet Homer wrote it around the eighth century BCE. The story is about a war between the people of Troy and the Greeks. Greek gods play a part too. While no dragons are in the story, the Greek king Agamemnon wears a blue dragon on his sword belt. This tells us that ancient Greeks were aware of dragons in the 700s BCE, even if just in stories.

This artwork shows the Greek god Zeus fighting with the dragon god Typhon.

Mount Etna, right, still erupts today!

IT'S A FACT!

The word "dragon" comes from the Greek word *drakōn*, which means "serpent." A serpent is another name for a large snake.

Roman author Pliny the Elder (23–79 CE) wrote a work called *Natural History*, which was 37 books in all. It was an encyclopedia of nature. Some of the books were about zoology, or the study of animals. While Pliny featured plenty of real creatures, he also wrote about some that weren't so real, such as headless people. Dragons, too, were included. For example, Pliny mentioned that Ethiopian dragons aren't as big as those in India. He also noted that dragons fight elephants and can choke them with their tails.

Do you think Pliny the Elder was describing real dragons in his *Natural History*?

Green tree python

Some think Pliny was actually writing about large snakes, such as pythons. But such snakes couldn't kill an elephant. They also don't grow as long as Pliny said dragons did. So what creature was Pliny the Elder writing about?

IT'S A FACT!

Pliny the Elder used the teachings of the Greek philosopher Aristotle (384–322 BCE) in his *Natural History*.

DRAGON REMEDIES

Pliny the Elder described remedies that can be made from various dragon parts in Book 29 of *Natural History*. For example, dragon "eyes, dried and beaten up with honey, form a liniment [ointment] which is an effectual preservative against the terrors of spectres [ghosts]." Other mixtures using dragon parts combined with other animals' parts were said to help people find "success in law-suits" and "repel [keep away] **venomous** creatures."

DRAGON SLAYERS

Some European tales focus not on dragons, but dragon slayers. Dragon slayers were portrayed, or represented, as brave heroes who won treasure, wisdom, or the love of a princess after killing a dragon. One of the most famous dragon slayer stories is about Saint George.

Saint George was a real person who lived around the third century CE. Many stories say he was a Roman soldier who died for his Christian faith. He was named a saint.

According to legend, Saint George traveled to the city of Silene in today's Libya, an African nation. He killed a dragon that was threatening the city and saved a princess. In thanks, the people there converted to Christianity. In this tale, the dragon is a symbol of evil. Saint George's courage and goodness helped him defeat it.

GEORGE AND PERSEUS

Some think the story of Saint George and the dragon was based on a Greek myth about Perseus, a son of Zeus. Perseus was traveling home from an adventure when he came across the princess Andromeda chained to a rock by the sea. To save his kingdom, Andromeda's father was giving her as a sacrifice to a sea monster, sometimes described as a sea dragon. Perseus killed the creature, saving the princess and her kingdom.

Saint George's symbol was a red cross on a white background. In England, people still wear Saint George costumes during certain celebrations. Some even dress as the dragon!

IT'S A FACT!

Although Saint George never visited England, his feast day, April 23, has long been a special day for the nation.

Beowulf was another legendary dragon slayer, though likely fictional. An unknown author in England wrote a famous epic poem about this **Scandinavian** hero, possibly around the eighth century.

In the story, the young Beowulf first defeated a swamp monster named Grendel and then Grendel's mother who sought to avenge her son. Beowulf became king of a place called Geatland, where he ruled peacefully for 50 years. In this kingdom, though, a dragon guarded a great treasure. One day, a thief stole some of the treasure, causing the furious dragon to begin to destroy Geatland. Beowulf fought the dragon, despite knowing that he would not survive the battle. Finally, he and another hero killed the creature, but not before Beowulf was bitten. After his death, Beowulf was buried next to the sea.

MONSTERS OF MANY NAMES

Many other kinds of dragon-like creatures exist in European legends. A basilisk is said to look like a huge snake or lizard. (Basilisks are real-life lizards too, though smaller than the legends!) A hydra is a water-dwelling monster that appears as a serpent with many heads. A wyvern is a two-legged dragon-like creature with wings. These aren't the only such mythic creatures. Is there some truth behind dragons that so many stories are told about them and similar creatures?

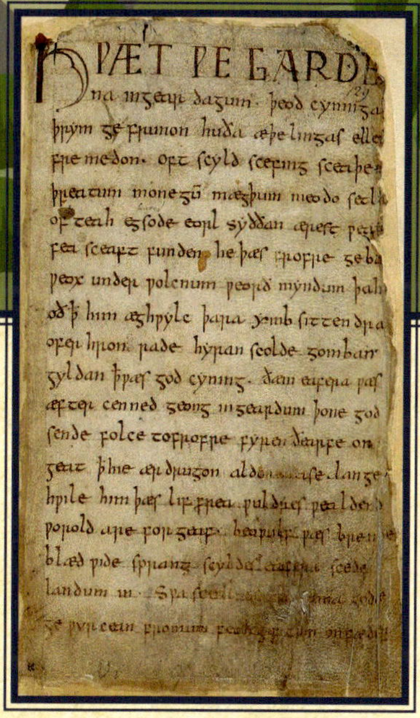

In the story of Beowulf, like other European dragon tales, Beowulf represents good, while the monsters he battles represent evil. The copy of *Beowulf* to the right is more than 1,000 years old.

IT'S A FACT!

Different authors have told the story of Beowulf many times over the centuries. The tale has been made into movies as well.

DRAGONS IN THE EAST

Europe isn't the only part of the world with dragon tales. Stories about dragons come from places in Asia too, including in Indian, Japanese, and Korean cultures. Dragons have remained important symbols in these places. Chinese culture is especially associated with dragons, and the connection is ancient. Carved dragons have been found at archaeological sites in China that date back as far as 4500 BCE!

Unlike dragons in European myths, the dragons in Chinese tales aren't cruel and evil. They're usually friendly to people and linked with good fortune. In Chinese stories, dragons often have the bodies and scales of snakes, four legs, horns, claws, and a large face with long whiskers and big eyes. Dragons were said to be able to change size and even disappear!

YIN AND YANG

The concept of yin and yang is essential to Chinese philosophy. This idea is about balance and harmony between opposites. Yin is water, cold, dark, the moon, valleys, and old, to name a few ideas. Yang is fire, heat, light, the sun, mountains, and young. A tiger represents yin, while a dragon represents yang. According to some, when yin and yang are out of balance—too much of one and not enough of the other—bad things can happen.

The dragon is one of the 12 animals of the **Chinese zodiac**. A person born under the sign of the dragon is said to have the qualities of a great leader.

IT'S A FACT!

In Chinese myths, a dragon may be called a *long* or *lung*.

Since dragons were connected with power, strength, and good luck in China, they were often symbols for important people, especially emperors. In fact, the dragon was considered to be the ruler of the animals just as the emperor ruled over his people.

Dragons of Chinese myth were closely connected to water. Many ancient people believed that dragons lived in water. Some Chinese rivers have the word "dragon" in their name for this reason. Some lore says that a dragon king lived in the four great seas of the world.

Some Chinese people believed dragons controlled the weather. Farmers asked dragons for rain for their crops. They wrote prayers on slips of paper or made offerings. Sometimes communities did dragon dances to bring rain or to heal someone.

DRAGONS TODAY

Dragons still decorate many rooftops, gardens, and buildings in China. In addition, the Dragon Boat Festival is held every year, with participants riding in boats carved and painted to look like dragons. Dragon dances are performed in many places where Chinese New Year is celebrated. People make long colorful dragon figures that seem to glide through the streets like giant serpents. This dance asks for good luck in the new year.

Some dragons in Chinese art are shown holding a pearl. The treasure likely represents wisdom and wealth.

IT'S A FACT!

Ancient Chinese emperors wore robes decorated with a dragon with five claws. It was believed less important dragons had just four claws.

Ryujin was a dragon king in Japanese myths. As a water god, he controlled the tide as well as rainfall and storms. It was said that he'd send snakes as messengers from his home, which was under the sea or in a volcano, depending on the story. Other stories state that Ryujin lived in Lake Biwa, near Kyoto, Japan.

In some lore, Ryujin helped people. He aided the hunter Hoori in finding a hook at the bottom of the sea, for example. But in another tale, Ryujin stole a jewel and hid it in his palace beneath the water, shown in the illustration above.

A building dedicated to Ryujin, called the Ryugu Shrine, is located in southern Japan. Some go there to pray for good fortune.

THE DRAGON KING

In Korean myths, the Dragon King Yongwang (or Yongsin) is a god of good health, harvest, and other areas of life. He was sometimes said to be a water god able to send rain to farms. He was also described as a god of fishermen who had control over wind and waves. He might be asked to help fishermen bring in a big catch, for example. In many stories, Yongwang lived in the underwater Yonggung (Dragon Palace).

Ryugu Shrine

Ryujin is believed to be one of eight dragon kings, tales of whom may have come from the mythology of India.

IT'S A FACT!

In Hindu mythology, which originated on the Indian subcontinent, the god Indra defeated the dragon Vritra, who **hoarded** rain and other water.

DRAGONS IN NORTH AMERICA

For centuries, inhabitants of ancient Mexico worshipped a god called Quetzalcóatl. He took many forms, sometimes a human man but often a creature that was a cross between a bird and snake. In fact, the name "Quetzalcóatl" means "**plumed** serpent." Doesn't that sound a bit like a dragon with feathers to you?

Different peoples believed this god controlled different parts of nature, but all thought he was powerful. The Aztecs who ruled central and southern Mexico in the fifteenth and sixteenth centuries believed Quetzalcóatl invented their calendar and books. He was also believed to be in the night sky in the form of the planet Venus.

OGOPOGO

Dragon sightings aren't just in ancient myths. A sea serpent is said to live in Okanagan Lake in British Columbia, Canada. Many people call the serpent Ogopogo. Some say it's a dragon-like beast with black or green skin. It has been reported to have the head of a horse, sheep, or snake. Others haven't seen it at all, but have observed mysterious waves in the lake that they think is Ogopogo just beneath the surface.

These are images of a temple in Teotihuacan, an ancient city near today's Mexico City. It is dedicated to Quetzalcóatl, the Aztec dragon-like god. Quetzalcóatl is pronounced keh-tzal-coh-WAH-tul.

IT'S A FACT!

The Syilx Okanagan People near Okanagan Lake have long respected a spirit of the water. Some people think this inspired the legend of Ogopogo.

REAL-LIFE DRAGONS?

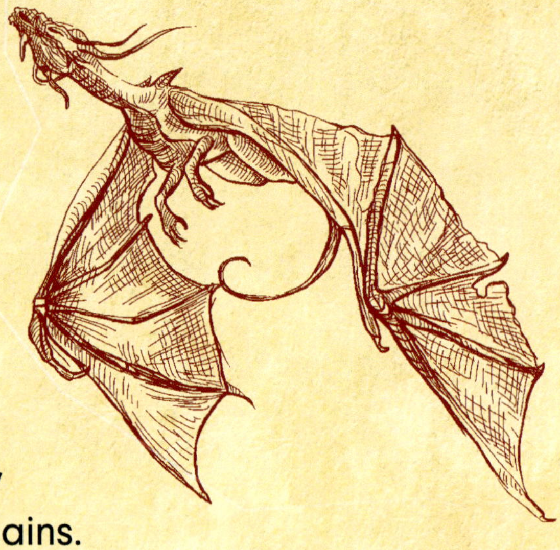

Many ancient peoples thought dragons were real. They prayed to them, feared them, and even sent them offerings. They saw dragons in nature too: in oceans, mountains, and clouds. When they uncovered large bones that had been buried in the earth, they sometimes thought they were dragon remains. Today, we know those were probably fossils of dinosaurs and other prehistoric animals. But it's easy to see how someone who knows nothing of such creatures would mistake the fossils for those of dragons.

For example, the fossils of the *Dracorex hogwartsia* look like they could have come from a dragon. They reveal that the dinosaur had a spiky head and walked on its back two legs. The dinosaur called *Zhenyuanlong* also looked like a dragon—with wings!

A THEORY

Some believe that accounts of dragons come from stories passed down from early humans who lived hundreds of thousands of years ago. These prehistoric people would have encountered animals that are now extinct, such as the giant monitor lizard (*Megalania*), which grew to be up to 25 feet (7.6 m) long. Descriptions passed down of such a creature from one generation to the next might have sounded much like descriptions of dragons.

The pterosaur, above, was a flying reptile. It lived long before people were on Earth. *Zhenyuanlong* is shown at left and *Dracorex* below.

IT'S A FACT!

Dracorex hogwartsia **is Latin for "dragon king of Hogwarts." Hogwarts is a school in the Harry Potter book series.**

Animals that still roam Earth might remind you of dragons, even if they're not large. One is found in the ocean. The leafy sea dragon is a fish related to the seahorse. It lives in waters near Australia. Leafy sea dragon bodies, which only grow to be about 1 foot (30 cm) long, are camouflaged as leaves.

The Gila monster of North America has a heavy scaly body, but only grows to be about 20 inches (51 cm) long. When this lizard bites, it clamps down and doesn't let go for several painful seconds. It's also venomous.

The Komodo dragon (illustration below) is much larger—it can be 10 feet (3 m) long. This monitor lizard, native to Indonesia, eats almost every part of an animal, even bones!

DEADLY REPTILES

Other reptiles that might have inspired dragon myths are the crocodile and alligator. These creatures live on land and in the water, and have massive mouths full of razor-sharp teeth. They're remarkably strong and will eat anything they can. Their long tails and scaly bodies could easily be mistaken for those of a small dragon. The largest crocodile found so far measured over 20 feet (6 m). The deadly creature lived in the Philippines where it attacked and killed people.

bearded dragon

leafy sea dragon

thorny devil

The bearded dragon is another kind of small lizard. Some are kept as pets. The thorny devil looks terrifying, but it's much too small to harm humans.

IT'S A FACT!

The thorny devil has spines—and a pretend extra head—to protect it from predators! It's also called the thorny dragon.

DRAGONS OF FICTION

Authors and filmmakers continue to tell stories about dragons. Some dragon characters are huge and terrifying. Others are small and cute. Both kinds appear in the popular How to Train Your Dragon book series and animated films about Vikings and their dragons.

J. R. R. Tolkien's *The Lord of the Rings* and *The Hobbit* books mention many fantasy creatures, including dragons and dragon-like monsters. J. K. Rowling's Harry Potter book series features at least 10 species of dragons, with names such as the Peruvian vipertooth and the Norwegian ridgeback. George R. R. Martin is the author of the book series A Song of Ice and Fire, which was the basis of the *Game of Thrones* TV series. Dragons are a key part of the action in the plot.

INSPIRED BY MYTH

Smaug—the dragon of J. R. R. Tolkien's *The Hobbit*—describes himself to the story's hero, Bilbo Baggins: "My armor is like tenfold shields, my teeth are swords, my claws spears, the shock of my tail a thunderbolt, my wings a hurricane, and my breath death!" Tolkien loved reading about dragons as a child and partly based Smaug on a dragon called Fafnir from Norse myths. Like Fafnir, Smaug hoarded treasure.

Here are a few famous dragons and where you can find them.

FAMOUS FICTIONAL DRAGONS

- MALEFICENT, *Sleeping Beauty* (movie)
- MUSHU, *Mulan* (movie)
- TOOTHLESS, *How to Train Your Dragon* (books and movies)
- FALKOR, *The NeverEnding Story* (movie)
- SAPHIRA, *Eragon* (book and movie)
- HAKU, *Spirited Away* (movie)
- *"PUFF THE MAGIC DRAGON"* (poem and song)
- ELLIOT, *Pete's Dragon* (movies)
- SMAUG, *The Hobbit* (book and movies)
- EUSTACE, *The Voyage of the Dawn Treader* (book and movie)

IT'S A FACT!

Fantasy is a kind of fiction that isn't based in a real-world setting. Many fantasy characters—such as dragons—are **supernatural**.

WHAT DO YOU BELIEVE?

Most people today don't believe in dragons. But what do you think? You've learned myths and legends about dragons and dragon-like creatures. These tales came from cultures in many parts of the world. How could ancient peoples who lived thousands of miles apart describe such similar creatures? Do you think there's a grain of truth behind the myths? Or do you think these accounts are based on discoveries of dinosaur bones or a story about an animal that was passed down over time?

Whether you believe dragons did exist and died out or you just can't believe such a creature ever lived, you must admit that people have never lost their interest in them. They continue to live on, at least in fiction. There's just something fascinating about dragons!

CRYPTIDS

Have you ever heard of cryptozoology? It's the study of animals that haven't been proven to exist yet. Cryptozoologists are people who try to figure out if these animals exist and may even search for them. (The prefix "crypt-" means "hidden.") Creatures that are legends until proven real are called cryptids. Some cryptids have been confirmed real over time, including the platypus, giant squid, and kangaroo. Do you think dragons could be added to this list someday?

Could dragons be hiding out in places humans can't get to?

IT'S A FACT!

A fire-breathing dragon-like creature called the Leviathan is described in the Book of Job in the Bible.

GLOSSARY

Chinese zodiac: a repeating 12-year cycle of animal signs and their assigned qualities, based on the lunar calendar

culture: a group of people that share beliefs and ways of life. Also, the beliefs and ways of life they share.

epic: a long form of poetry that tells the story of a legendary or historical hero

hoard: to collect a supply of something and hide it from others

lore: traditional stories, knowledge, or beliefs about a certain location, group, or subject that are passed down

plumed: having the feathers of a bird

Scandinavian: from the region of northern Europe called Scandinavia now occupied by Norway, Sweden, and Denmark. Sometimes Scandinavia also includes Iceland and Finland.

supernatural: unable to be explained or seeming to come from magic

talon: one of a bird's sharp claws

temperament: nature, or usual mood or behavior

underworld: in mythology, the place where souls go after death

venomous: able to produce a liquid called venom that is harmful to other animals

FOR MORE INFORMATION

BOOKS

Loh-Hagan, Virginia. *Dragons*. Ann Arbor, MI: Cherry Lake Publishing, 2017.

Macfarlane, Tamara. *Dragon World*. New York, NY: DK Children, 2021.

Wilkinson, Philip. *Myths, Legends & Sacred Stories: A Visual Encyclopedia*. New York, NY: DK Publishing, 2019.

WEBSITES

Ancient China: Mythology

www.ducksters.com/history/china/chinese_mythology.php

Find out more about Chinese myths—dragons included!

Britannica Kids: Dragon

kids.britannica.com/students/article/dragon/274056

Discover more dragon stories told throughout history here.

The Legend of Saint George and the Dragon

projectbritain.com/stgeorge2.html

Read more about the famous legend.

INDEX